Kittens and Puppies

Ladybird

purring kitten

playful puppy

bouncy lamb

pink piglet

yellow duckling

naughty fox cub

hopping joey

silky seal pup

fluffy chick

tufty owlet

skipping foal

friendly calf

cuddly bear cub

stripy zebra foal

splashing whale calf

furry kid

feathery cygnet

growling lion cub

leaping dolphin calf

soft gosling

chirpy penguin chick

grey elephant calf

baby gorilla

wiggly tadpoles